What's for lunch?

Rice

Library of Congress Catalogiing-in-Publication Data
Robson, Pam
  Rice / written by Pam Robson. --1st American ed.
  p. cm. -- (What's For Lunch?)
  Includes index.
  Summary: Follows rice from its source on farm or plantation right
through to the table discussing how rice is grown, processed, and produced.
  ISBN 0-516-20824-1
  1. Rice--Juvenile literature. 2. Rice products--Juvenile
literature. [1. Rice.] I. Title II. Series: Robson, Pam.
What's for Lunch?
SB191.R5R65 1997   97-6041
641.3'318--dc21   CIP
                                         AC

© 1997 Franklin Watts
96 Leonard Street
London
EC2A 4RH

First American edition 1998 by
Franklin Watts
A Division of Grolier Publishing
Sherman Turnpike
Danbury, CT 06816

ISBN 0-516-20824-1 (lib. bdg.)
ISBN 0-516-26224-6 (pbk)

Editor: Samantha Armstrong
Designer: Kirstie Billingham
Consultant: Professor Paul Davies
Reading Consultant: Prue Goodwin, Reading and Language
Information Centre, Reading

Printed in Hong Kong

What's for lunch?

Rice

Pam Robson

CHILDREN'S PRESS®

A Division of Grolier Publishing

LONDON • NEW YORK • HONG KONG • SYDNEY
DANBURY, CONNECTICUT

Today we are having rice for lunch.
The rice we eat is usually white
but it can also be brown, red, or black.
Rice is full of **starch**.
Eating rice gives you **energy**.

The rice plant is a kind of grass.

It grows best when it is mostly under water.

So rice is planted in fields
that are flooded with water.

These are called **paddy** fields.

Some rice is grown on hillsides
that are cut into **terraces**.

Rice is grown in countries where it is hot
and there is plenty of rain.
In some places, farmers use machines
to help them grow their rice.
In other places, people do most of the work.

The plant grows
from **grains** of rice.
The grains grow into
green **seedlings.**
Farmers plant the seedlings
in the paddy fields.

Farmers water the rice plants
to help them grow.
They put **fertilizer**
on the fields
to make the plants strong.
Insects sometimes eat the rice.
The farmers use **insecticide**
to kill the insects.

Little flowers called **spikelets**
appear on the plant.
The grains of rice grow inside the spikelets.
Each grain is protected by a tough outside layer
called a **husk** and a skin of **bran.**

When the plants turn golden,
the rice is ready to **harvest**.
The farmers cut down the plants.
They separate the grains of rice from the plants.
This is called **threshing**.
Sometimes animals walk on the plants
to separate the grains of rice.

Next the farmers remove the husks
from the grains of rice.
A machine blows the husks away.
This is called **winnowing**.
Sometimes this is done in a factory.

At this stage the grains of rice
still have a layer of bran around them.
This is called brown rice.

The bran can be removed.
This is called **polishing**.
Underneath the rice is white.

The rice is packed into sacks
and taken to shops and markets
where it is sold.
Some rice has a longer journey.
It is loaded onto ships and taken
to other countries to be sold.

There are many different types of rice.
Grains of rice can be long,
medium, or short.
In India long grain rice
is eaten with curry.

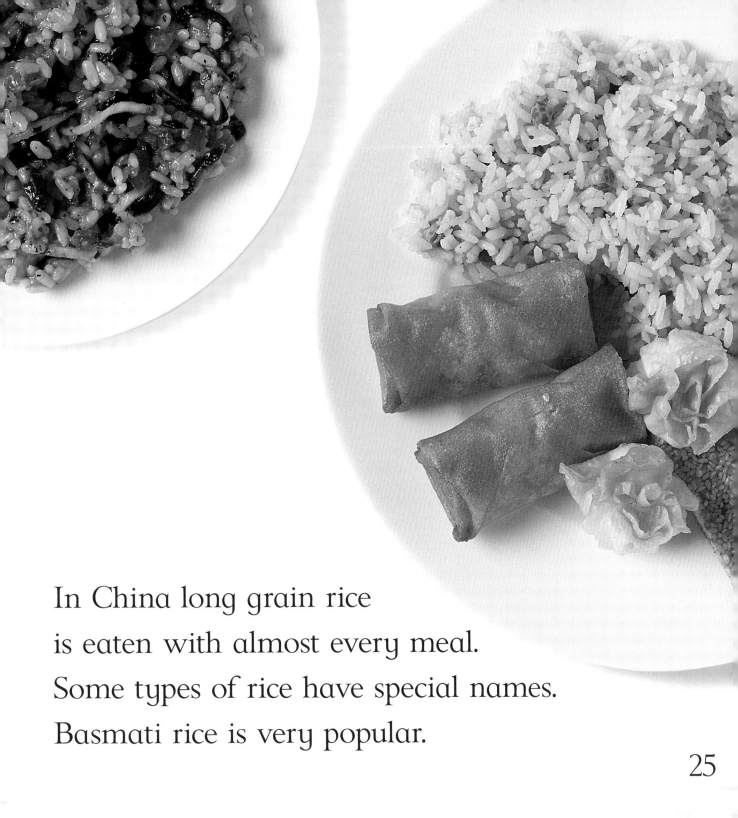

In China long grain rice
is eaten with almost every meal.
Some types of rice have special names.
Basmati rice is very popular.

Rice can be cooked in many different ways.
It can be steamed and toasted
and used to make breakfast cereal.

People eat rice all over the world.
In China people use chopsticks
to eat their rice.
In India rice is sometimes
served on banana leaves.
For many people rice is
a very important food.

Glossary

bran the brown skin of a grain of rice

energy the strength to work and play

fertilizer something that helps plants grow

grain the small hard part of a grass that looks like a seed

husk the outside covering of a grain of rice

insecticide something that kills insects

paddy fields that are flooded with water

polishing removing the bran layer from rice to make it into white rice

seedling a very young plant that grows from a seed

spikelet the flower of the rice plant

starch something that gives you energy

terrace	a flat area that is cut into a hill
threshing	separating the grains of rice from the plants
winnowing	blowing away the husks from the grains of rice

Index

Picture credits: Eye Ubiquitous 28 (David Cumming); Holt Studios 8 (Inga Spence), 9 (S.B.G. McCullagh), 13 (Nigel Cattlin), 14 (Nigel Cattlin), 16 (Inga Spence), 18-9 (D. Donne Bryant), 23 (Inga Spence); Robert Harding 6 (Gavin Hellier), 10 (T. Megarry), 15 (Gavin Hellier); Panos Pictures 7 (Guy Mansfield), 12 (Alain le Garsmeur), 17 (Peter Barker), 22 (Jeremy Hartley). Nick Bailey Photography cover, 3, 5; All other photographs Tim Ridley, Wells Street Studios. **With thanks to Jessica Hopf and Lois Browne.**